to liv

GW01451461

Ananya Prabhullan

BookLeaf
Publishing
India | USA | UK

Presentation by *BookLeaf Publishing*

Web: www.bookleafpub.com

E-mail: info@bookleafpub.com

ISBN: 9789358736205

First edition 2023

DEDICATION

Dear Primary Rat,

This book is for you. I hope this makes up a bit for how unkind I have been to you over the years when all you've done is nurture and nourish us. You dreamt of big things, and you believed in us. It got lost somewhere along the way, but I promise we will find it together. Thank you for laughing always, for loving, believing and protecting this little heart of ours. I love you, you silly little brown rat.

Love

Ananya

ACKNOWLEDGEMENT

To God, my faith in you keeps me rooted.

My loving parents, beloved Gran, Kee, and grandparents, for imparting wisdom and love that flow through my veins, shaping the essence of my words. You all are my guiding light and pillars of strength, and without you, I am nobody.

To my sweet babies, Candy and Neo, my eternal muses, and the keepers of my heart. You both hold the last remnants of my childhood in your gentle souls.

To my handsome cat brother, Benjamin Prabhullan, thank you for being my loyal companion and keeping me company through the quiet nights of writing.

To my dearest friends, you are my chosen family. I cannot begin to think of what my life would be without you dears. I wish you all the success and peace this world can offer and then a bit more.

To all who have patiently endured my moments of confusion and silliness, thank you for your unwavering patience.

To Book Leaf Publishing, you've turned the impossible into reality, and I'm immensely grateful for your dedication and hard work.

To the world, thank you.

2023-21: to live is to sin

I)

I am not selfless

Though I do not suffer in the flesh

I am tormented

Forevermore submerged

In agony's putrid spill

Of a relentless dark mind

Forevermore lamenting

Of suffering's torment and how it has tormented

II)

Each morning my tongue seeks out

Hastily for the remnants
Before I can moisten my lips

In the ashy rum

While my brutish locks

Lay damp kissing moonlight farewell

For as I continue to exist in time

Conscience and breath repeated

She will be there, colourful and hazy

For it is important

Participation in devouring etiquette

With her encouragement that captivates me

In his and hers most banal conversations

And most trite of them all, my prosaic musings

And yet I justify and defend

Travesty of self one after the other

For if I had courage
Would I not reheat morsels frozen in the middle?

And cease sermonising

Of callous existence

more nauseating than harrowing suffering

III)

This pain

Chases me

indefatigably on my deathbed

Clusters of attachments clump

An assemblage of that which was and could be

Yet I say with no jest

To have a priest if I ever were so lucky

A person or two if I ever were so blessed

To eulogise my shortcomings
Commemorate my lies

And scrutinise my tenderest of tears

After all, if there is suffering, should there not be
a cause

And if there is a cause

What is the end for this lifetime

And this lifetime only?

mirth askew

It is through love that I am humourless

For what is humour deluged in the pain of a
lover's distress

You deny humour begrudges love,

Revelry disguised in jealousy's shove

You deny humour is bloodthirsty

As if there is love and then insecurity

But why don't you ease his garrotte

If my lover must not hurt, must not discredit

For I realised I had never breathed

Until I drowned in his smile, momentarily freed

My expectations of love are far greater than the actual reality

But my lover is my only truth and he cures me of my mortality

I rest in the plane between life and death

And I need my lover so I may pass through life's length

He paints me with life and he quells my soul

For in him lies death's console

Pity is crueller than hope

Is that why you were silent when I first spoke

And asked you once and again

Why my lover leaves in pain

There can't be pain in shame

But I know my lover loves, shrouded in secretive flame

When does separation's purgation end,

If it were ever beheld

I miss my lover's warmth

Snug in the winter north

I miss my lover's lies

In his most sincere sighs

For my lover is true in my love for him

In his lips, his eyes, his chuckle and furtive hymn

He speaks not then of a barren love

So I ask you, you from above

Why is there comfort in suffering

Why is there respite in longing

They're all out to besiege and inflict
My lover by them, in agony, to permit

When I look at my lover's closed eyes

It is free of scrutiny, it does not chastise

So I gape at his still eyes lovingly

His scent, his embrace, lulling me

When he plants a kiss swiftly, amongst reticent
denies

my heart melts and my soul cries

And his dismay at loving me,

Keeps me nourishingly chained and agonised

As if we lost a revolution and we are now
revolutionised

If you from above sent me my lover

I shall never ask you for another

He's been my first and he is my last

And I wonder with my lover, will death ever last?

For I'd rather take not another, and die

In his hands and under the rose sky

Over his deep breaths and sweet kisses

He mumbles, low and vicious

If only I were pretty, if only I were better, he sermonises

Why did you forget to say love was scrutiny beneath ruby horizons

I tell you, in beseeched whisper

That he held me close over-possessive purrs

In the solitude of dawn by the river

My lover yearned and I was her

And I ask you,

Submerged in blood, darker than his hue

If a lover's hilarity

Lies in the tender slumber of barbarity

poor cousin

In a world of equals,

I'm the poor cousin, blessed

for a seat at the banquet

among god-fearing men.

The darker sister, jubilant,

with barely a hint

of the dotted red, loved

in degrees by her pagan gods—

where feasts not for the hungry,

but rewarded by birth.

Through talks, politely circled away,

I'd never seen linen so crisp,
glinting in the candlelight,

and wool so soft, embracing

the dark corner I was seated at,

amidst those further up,

where my opinion is politely ignored,

whispered, audibly thrice to their ears.

This is the new world—

they say, things are not as bad,

Nobody discriminates—how things change, they
wonder.
Fatalistic? Just humour
Complexity? Unnecessary

Home sweet home,

I came not forced, but pleaded

against ambition's dismissal,

forgetting that soon, I'll be neither here nor
there.

I can blame neither,

they both look at my skin,

my birth, and femininity.

The aroma of my spices,

too pungent, they say,

still lingers,

as the sweat of my blood existed

before your nations,

and the sweat of this lifetime

is for all our children.

vase

I was given a vase once,

told when older

I would inherit it

in its glass case.

The vase was not as pretty as the ones in books,

It was not as tall or finely made,

There were cracks towards the neck, negligible
unless traced

The vase had two handles, stretching an inch into our home,

I had never seen a vase with two handles, messily attached,

trapped, never to freely roam

Unsymmetrical, with an almost goofy face.

The vase was brown near its shoulder and belly,

Shades of brown journeying to the base.

There was nothing special about the vase,

It was crafted by an ancestor

and was left for me and maybe my offspring

When I was older

I snatched it from my family and stole her

A reminder of the home I had left forever

not that nostalgia could ever

hinder someone this clever

During days, I fling her to the side

on shoddy windowsills

or over piles of cloth spills

During nights I sit beside

A tweezer in hand

brooding over

the absence of paints and frills

Wet eyes replaced with tweezers

to fix, change and paint

I didn't know what

I had never been taught

In anger, every night

I soak it in water
slowly carving

scraping, grazing and gouging

soft earth, sticky, crumbly, seeps between my
fingers

As I crush chunks of it,

the juice of silly aspirations

its hue no longer cascades.

I no longer go home

Because I am reminded

of the toasty caramel vase

I was once promised, once given

the same hues of the earth

the same dreams as that of a child

I look at the crumbled dust near the foot of the
vase

I look at the wilted petals

still under the dirty piles of cloth

a souvenir.

dear father

Monologue after monologue

my eyes glaze over the empty mental coliseum

unmoved at discourses of casual destruction

never fulfilling the promise of an epilogue

And yet, I am too daunted to pen

of purity, divinity and misconstruction

too daunted to pen

about the disquietude, the base

of my father and his father's trace

chambered subdued smiles of fortune

dwindled and scarce since my grandfather's birth

worn out, as the hands obey over again
bridled in service and duty

And so I am too daunted to pen

of my father and the little boy within

silent, keen-eyed

with his older brother, in small knickers,

racing around, calling out to each other

picking up fallen blossoms of konnapoo

the golden blossoms of pookalam

remind me of my father

And so I am too daunted to pen

because I fear

I stain the purity of youth

with the rottenness of my filth
away from their blood, through my sin

In another universe

I am young

I am happy and I embrace my father

my god, much larger than life

and his feet will no longer ache,

while I place the blanket he'd once

meticulously cover my childhood in

over his tired shoulders

and I will grow worthy of his love.

mumbai (माझे शहर, माझी जबाबदारी)

My neon city of the common,

the brave, and the rich,

spread across

like green bangles

received as prasad.

My neon city of song,

clinks in raw melody,

khaki motor warriors

zoom in front of houses—

hearts big and tales tall

My neon city of survivors,

where I don't belong,

among the persistent and willed,

the selfless and self-effacing

for my local train-

has no rhythm

My neon city of extremes,

matchbox riches

and crammed chawls

where the modest and sensible

are both the rulers and servers.

womanhood

accusations hurt more

when it's the long feminine fingers

belonging to the unkohled eyes.

which collapse into a cruel line

while an unmatching smile dances

dangerously across her face

a tango of repulsion

accusatory and perverse wonderment

'Women know women'

do I reflect

like a lustrous mirror

your deepest desire
or do you mirror

your cryptic performances

through me?

I wonder,

amidst the ache inside

we are born of the earth's blood

sisters may bicker

but blood never hates

thirst

I stare at him
no longer delicious
there is no aroma

he is defiled
in the shadow of morning dew
fragrant decay

he laughs merrily
my beautiful death
so succulent

'forgive me'
shiver and recoil
from his curdled breath

my baby is rotting
wounds ooze burgundy clots
lofty kisses twinkle

I lay by him
purple fingers clenched
palate finally sophisticated

global citizen

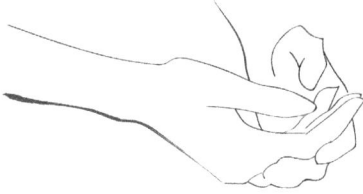

I realised I had perished

when their words affected me more

than those of my countrymen

For I had begun to be like them

and thought of them as my own

and each pointed remark

stabbed into conversations

remind me that I will never be theirs

and now I have lost

those of my own

motherland

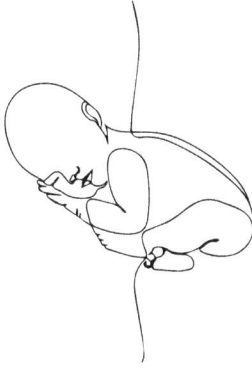

I pine for the warmth of my mother

the colours of the ocean in her saree,

her embrace like the purring of the sea

different hues of the sun reflected in her gold
necklace

the crescent earring spread around her lobe

I pine for the warmth of my mother

her long, almond-cool fingers,

patting my back, lulling me into sleep

I pine for the warmth of my mother

I pine for the warmth of my motherland

Just as my motherland is a tribute to life

I visit the graves,

the tombs of those of my blood I have never met

A grandfather I once chanced upon

resting now in a graveyard

tomb after grave

grave after tomb

perhaps it is an irony of sorts

an irreverent joke about death

After all the garden of death

is more of an odyssey

of once what existed

remembered momentarily by those in the flesh,

decorated by the hands of those who love

in memory and guilt.

I pine for the warmth of my mother

each farewell, I solemnly photograph her

but I will forever remember her

as my mother when I was ten

Long, luscious hair, mischief in her toothy grin

hand in hand with father,

as I'd run to play in the night, deeper than her
hair.

almond eyes

The daughter grows up

owing to wrestle

through the tethers

mothers and daughters

chained like animals

'I have never been my mother's tan fawn

but blossom from the seed of my father's forest'

Then why is she ensnared

in the same chains of anger

Then why is she grappling
in the same chains of suffering

like her mother and the women before her?

hi diya, it's me again...

(A letter from 2019 I never sent, converted into haikus in 2023)

Tears trace cheeks like paint,

Self-disgust concealed in guise,

Charade veils the truth.

Back, stomach entwine,

Dragon scars bind skin, outlines,

Thighs, cylinder wide.

Dear Diya, can truth

Shape self amidst world's whispers?

Liar's fate derides.

Dear Diya, I see,

Memories as dragonflies flee,

Again anew, nymphs

Crystal wings embrace,

Dragonflies in skies they soar,

Soil yet claims dreams' trace.

Crystallized wings hold,

Helplessness in tales untold,

Must go, time takes hold.

Tears unshed, I'll embrace,

Nose pinched, mask I will place now

As I bid farewell

2018-2016 (Poetry Hiatus and its result-) i could write before

I miss how comforting it used to be before

Now all I do is try more and more

Words don't come out easily

Not like how they used to before

I don't have anything to say or convey

But I could write before.

Each syllable feels forced.

My hands are clenching my mind between two rocks; the blood writhes out like the gait of a slow blaise snake.

It was not like this before,

words would flow through me; not from within but into the deepest and smallest pore of my being

like the illusioned straight rays of the moon do into the inner depths of a lake.

I can't write now when I'm the saddest and I can't write now when I'm the happiest,

For my soul seems blank.

But I could write before.

I could write whatever was asked of me.

But now I can feel- I just feel.

My sanity seems to be leaving me,

Unearthing the depreciable wreck shrouded behind the clay mask

But the clay is cracking,

Under heat-under pressure- under expectations

Oh! How fine we are made,

Our bare souls wrapped in bandages before clay masks,

Like our soul is a fragile artefact.

Are we concealing or are we protecting?

Ourselves or the world outside?

I am but human, so I believe

I have hope

that I might still be able to revert to before.

But belief has lie embedded in it.

So, words don't come out easily

Not like how they used to before,

But I could write before.

true love

[1] I know not of your love

But I know of mine and that is enough

For the both of us

[2] The waves inch closer

Must you flounder, O Love, in telling my being
of our love?

My soul knows but my heart does not.

[3] Show haste O love,

Let us escape from this weary ploy they call the world

Let us soar from this inconsequential slight

[4] Where is the warmth my heart lacks?

[5] (In Science Class)

The only thing innovation leads to is more failure and higher disappointments

Just like teenage, the pinnacle of

bad times and self-hatred

at least it's supposed to get better

[6] Hatred makes me steam with anger, helplessness and exhaustion.

I feel like a worm,

Trapped in a glass jar,

tired of the incessant poking continuing on my lifeless, impaled body.

[7] It does not matter if all I have for you is fleeting

or, if it is an emotion strong enough to crush mountains.

What I do know,

however,

is that all I need and want right now is you.

2015-2013- benevolence

In talks of love, hope, and kindness's grace,

Lies a solemn serenity of lies untold,

Born from dire generations, deep and thoughtful,

Taut circumstances and idle existence's hold.

Expressed through kind inquiries and words'
embrace,

Fulfillment's common thread selfishly spun,

Starting at shared points, journey's trace,

Need and want align, two lives as one.

where needful and wantful are one,

the giving, the needful; the receiver the
salvation.

the path

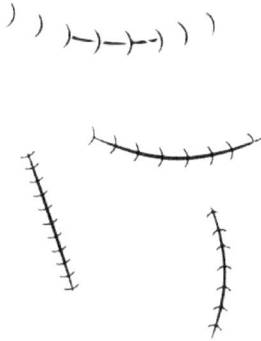

The somber delights of crossroads high

Or the sudden dismay at choosing one

Another page, another word

O'er again and furthermore

A path is taken, a path is chosen

Like the tip of leaves to the tip of roots

A fine line between the two

Unique to the other, unique to his own self

One path – one parallel destiny

Till oh! The choice is no more yer

awakening

Those halcyon times seem so far

It is now an incomprehensible impugn.

Useless were all those fights, the brawls we had
to par,

Everything lost – everything in a ruin.

Nowhere to go, nowhere to be.

Light sprinkling through the thin crack,

Close my eyes and turn away.

It's too late, turn away—

I'm already lost, the world hired like a claque.

The crack widens, the light pours in.

'Go away,' I croak, 'It's over.'

The voices inside quieten down—there now is
no din.

They seem bent upon saving her—

Saving me.

The light soon fades. The voices return,

'Why?' I cry, 'Why didn't you help?'

I've fallen deeper. There is nothing else to learn,
no one to help.

The light has completely disappeared like the
trails of a recidivist.

The plunge has meaning now.

This is my destiny—I am the forgotten mist.
The coup de grâce.

I'm leaving now and going far-far away,

Life seems like a miserable farce.
Save me, I implore, I'll do anything for that ray.

This was a mistake! Give me one last say.

A voice speaks warm but frigid,

Near but far.

'I offered you my hand but you pushed me livid.

I pulled you forward but you went back.'

I groan and ask, 'Who are you?'

'I'm the piece that binds you.

I'm your bad and I'm your good.

You've suppressed me long enough.

It's time to drop that knife.

You've killed your old self.

You're now consecrated.

You must understand that life is a little rough,

But you mustn't aim the trigger at life.
Awake, you are not yet sated.

Life is no ride, it is no game,

For everybody, it's not the same.'

'Will you leave me now?' I whispered.

'How can I leave you when I am you and you
are me?'

just a dream

"Mother, what if this all is just a dream?

What if the sun doesn't shine in reality

and birds have money to purchase oranges?"

asked the half-asleep child,

already wading towards that night's dream.

Each tick of the cuckoo clock reminded each
one of us

what we had to redeem.

"Now dear one," the mother crooned,

"Go to sleep or else all your dreams will pile."

The child slept, but the world kept buzzing onward,

for, on the other side, a child had woken up.

"Ma," she asked, "What if the world is just a dream?

What if we are not real?"

Not surprised by her child's question,

The mother said, "Then I wouldn't want it to end.

I couldn't bear to live in a world without you."

Far away, where dusk was approaching,

a girl asked her father,

"Pa, what if this world is just a dream?"

He smiled jovially and chuckled,

"Well, it's a jolly good one now, ain't it?"

A little further where the owl feasted,

A girl looked into the mirror and asked the looking glass,

"What if this world is just a horrible dream?"

The glass was cracked, she noticed.

The girl on the other side was nowhere to be found.

All she could see were people wielding pitchforks and fire.

They cried out loud, "Wake up—wake up!"

Startled with fright, the girl jumped out of her sheets.

The world had stopped, her chest heaved hard.

Which is the façade—the present or the past?

last leaf (O.Henry)

(reimagined from the perspective of Johnsy)

I lay in my wilted glen

Few may say a sick bed

Shielded from the voice of men

I hear nothing but the wind said

I lay in my wilted glen

Force-fed hot broth and soup

Slowly disappearing in my defeated den

I have given up all hope

I had a dream

To create the Bay of Naples

To be part of the crème de la crème

To dance among the maples

It all faded away at once

The cold choking fingers pressed against my throat

It consumed my very soul

It brought back my thoughts of loath

Life seems so futile

A drunken abyss and nothing more

Defeat and disappointments all pile

All that I can hear is the Grim Reaper's roar

The leaves are falling,

One at a time

My soul linked to the creeper climbing

Brings forth

The harmony of my last breath and the last leaf

amy

Inebriated in her sordid reverie,

rudely awoken by the world around.

They seared her faith and scorched her heart;

A tragic event, concealed in darkness,

by the world's silence.

No blame, no burden.

Before giving up, she thought,

"Do you really want to do this, Amy?"

But the world closed in; escape was survival.

Some other time, she thought.

The world was startled, shocked.

By the mantle, they stood,

"She was happy; what went wrong with her?"
they wondered.

A deep breath, then they said,

"She had closed her walls, pushed us away."

Sipping from water glasses, they added,

"If she had let us help, she would still be here."

Seated in armchairs, they exclaimed,

"She was always a little different."

Taking cookies, they reminisced,

"An emotional menace, cribbing all night,

about how upset she was."

Yawning, they remarked,

"She brought it upon herself."

Like seasons, thoughts shift.

Amy was no more,

nor was her memory.

ere

She stood betwixt bewail and bicker,

A wise erudite by thought and manner.

Ere was the time of honour and pride,

Espalier she was then taught to grow long and slide.

Came along was a Spaniard, his robes flying strong,

He took her to a world of fantasy and song.

The times spent were nought but joy and elation,

Till suddenly he left, thus ending their relation.

Oh! How she sobbed and poured her soul

on the banks by the willow.
Her heart broken, torn and hollow,

Oh! How he came like a wrecking hurricane,

Dancing ere with her in the rain.

Days passed as her heart yearned for him,

She stood by the docks till the sun grew dim.

Her pining soul reaching out for him,

'Come back' to be heard was her only hymn.

She waited for him far beyond the docks,

Alas! He was naught but a faux.

She stood by the docks for the last time,

Last she heard was the church bells chime.

She plunged into darkness,
Enveloping her petite body in harshness.
Her silver cascade billowing in the currents,

In the end, unwisely she gave into the word of
defeat.

Forgo her life, she did for that cheat,

Disappearing deep into the torrents.

an ode to my true love

(My darling candy,

If you're reading this, always remember that I have loved you and always will do so. I think about you every second of my life. When I smile, I wonder why you're not there to share it with me. Why are you not the sole reason for my happiness? When I see beauty I remember your beauty. You were not one who thought of grace but you are my queen. You are the reason I exist. Seeing you come makes my heart leap, I lose control of life. When I speak to you, time is not something I care for. The moon reminds me of your beauty whereas the sun reminds me of your smile.

A day without you is like a year without
pedigree You may never love me but always
remember, I do.

-A poem written by a Neapolitan mastiff for a
girl Labrador)

You are my one true love
To fall in love with you took only a fleeting
glance
You are Aphrodite's dove I tried making an
advance towards your heart
But your weary eyes told me no,
They told me you had to attend to your duties
Chasing a crow
Or driving a cat up a tree But it made me moody
I brought you many a froggy
I swore to you truly

You are my light
My path out of darkness

You steer me away from harshness
For not doing bad you are my knight

But I strayed away
I fell for the reeds
You surfaced and gave me your paws
You taught me the ways of "woof"

But when the talk of our love was mentioned,
you turned aloof
You glared at me
Anger flared
We parted

I couldn't stop thinking about you
Your hazel eyes filled with mirth
You are the dearth of my life
Maybe it is my drool you are disgusted with
But I don't mind
For I still pine

You threatened me with a twig-shaped knife
Growling you will kill me if I come near
My body turns rigid with fear
But my heart still loves

-A pining Neapolitan Mastiff

Milton Keynes UK
Ingram Content Group UK Ltd.
UKHW021945010924
447661UK00012B/687

9 789358 736205